# Kitchen & Bathroom

Cy DeCosse Incorporated
Minnetonka, Minnesota

# Contents

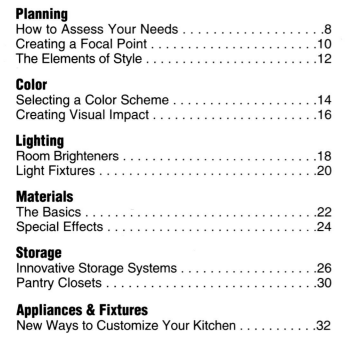

Copyright © 1994
Cy DeCosse Incorporated
An Imprint of Cowles Creative Publishing
5900 Green Oak Drive
Minnetonka, Minnesota 55343
1-800-328-3895
All rights reserved
Printed in U.S.A.

Creative Publishing

*A Division of Cowles Enthusiast Media, Inc.*

*President/COO:* Nino Tarantino
*Executive V.P./Editor-in-Chief:*
  William B. Jones

Library of Congress
Cataloging-in-Publication Data

Kitchen & bathroom ideas.

p. cm.—(Black & Decker home improvement library)
ISBN 0-86573-738-X
1. Kitchens.
2. Bathrooms.
3. Interior decoration.
I. Cy DeCosse Incorporated.
II. Title: Kitchen and bathroom ideas.
III. Series
NK2117.K5K55   1994
747.7'8—dc20

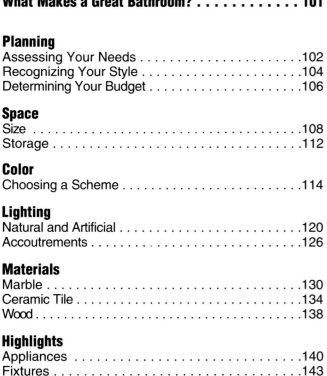

*Created by:* The Editors of Cowles Creative Publishing, in cooperation with Black & Decker. **BLACK&DECKER** is a trademark of the Black & Decker Corporation and is used under license.

Also available from the publisher:
*Everyday Home Repairs, Decorating With Paint & Wallcovering, Carpentry: Tools•Shelves•Walls•Doors, Kitchen Remodeling, Building Decks, Home Plumbing Projects & Repairs, Basic Wiring & Electrical Repairs, Workshop Tips & Techniques, Advanced Home Wiring, Carpentry: Remodeling, Landscape Design & Construction, Bathroom Remodeling, Built-in Projects for the Home, Refinishing & Finishing Wood, Exterior Home Repairs & Improvements, Home Masonry Repairs & Projects, Building Porches & Patios*

*Creative Director:* William B. Jones
*Project Director:* Paul Currie
*Art Directors:* Tim Himsel, Gina Seeling
*Project Manager:* Diane Dreon
*Copy Editor:* Janice Cauley
*Staff Photographer:* Mike Parker
*Production Staff:* Carol Harvatin, Tracy Stanley, Julie Sutphen
*Print Production Coordinator:* Linda Halls

COWLES
Enthusiast Media

*President/COO:* Philip L. Penny

*Printed on American paper by:*
R. R. Donnelley & Sons Co.
99 98 97 96 / 5 4 3 2 1

# Kitchen Ideas

# What Makes a Great Kitchen?

A great kitchen is one that is made just for your family. It is a comfortable, attractive and efficient place in which to work and socialize. Simply put, a great kitchen is a room your family loves.

To help you plan your great kitchen, we have assembled more than 150 color photographs of outstanding kitchen designs and features.

The first section of this book shows how you can customize your kitchen to reflect your family's life-style and tastes. It highlights the elements of a great kitchen: interesting color schemes, unique building materials, creative lighting, space-expanding storage units, and unusual appliances and fixtures.

The second section has more than 50 pages filled with pictures of fantastic kitchens. Included are all the classic styles, ranging from traditional to country to contemporary. We have also added the "inspirational-style" kitchen. This innovative style lets you step beyond the usual boundaries of design and decor to create your own personal look.

Whether you are sprucing up your old kitchen, planning a major overhaul, or designing a completely new kitchen, this book is sure to give you plenty of useful ideas.

Photo courtesy of Dura Supreme

**Style.** *Classic country features such as massive beams and rustic accessories mix well with contemporary tile countertops and flooring. Select a classic kitchen style—country, traditional, contemporary — then give it a personal accent.*

Photo courtesy of Interplan Design Corp. photographed by DOMIN

**Focal point.** *Elegant brass range hood steals the show in this understated contemporary kitchen. Select one stunning feature, material or color, and make it the center of the kitchen plan.*

Photo courtesy of KraftMaid Cabinetry, Inc.

**Color.** *Buy a lot of style on a little budget. Accent a neutral scheme with bold, bright accessories, as in this white and red kitchen. A monochromatic color plan is soothing; high-contrast colors are lively and energizing.*

**Light.** *Warm daylight floods the sink area; electric fixture brightens the cooking alcove. Combine natural and electrical lighting in the kitchen plan.*

**Storage.** *Pantry has adjustable wire baskets that will accommodate most containers. Swinging panels allow access to back shelves. For efficient storage, use vertical as well as horizontal space.*

**Materials.** *Rich cabinetry, eye-catching tile and floral wallcovering give this kitchen the feel of spring. The more creative the mix of materials, the more unique the kitchen style.*

**Detail.** *Art Deco kitchen is rich in detail. Curved cabinets and graceful flowers define the period style. Deco colors—peach and green—unify the design.*

# Planning

## Fit your life-style

Kitchen planning starts with a close look at your family. How large is it? Is your family growing? Consider your family's eating and cooking habits. Who eats at home? How often? Does your family eat together? Where?

Think over these questions, too: How much cooking is done each week? Is there more than one cook? Are fresh or prepared foods more important? How often is equipment like a wok, griddle, food processor or pasta maker used? The answers to these questions will help you select appliances and estimate the food and equipment storage space needed.

Include socializing in this life-style inventory. Does your family enjoy entertaining? How often? Where? For how many guests? Is entertaining informal or formal? Do guests help with kitchen duties? A floor plan begins to emerge as you consider how the kitchen relates to the entertaining areas.

Also list special family needs, such as space for a laundry, a sewing and ironing area, a phone center, a hobby counter or seating for children.

***Plan a home office.*** *Keep tabs on business from a space-saving kitchen work station. For a unified look, match desk and counter-top materials. Here, a computer center in peach and oyster laminate duplicates cabinet and counter materials.*

***Plan a play area.*** *Baby is safe in a fenced play yard while Mom or Dad tackles kitchen chores. Plan a carpeted area, located out of the traffic pattern, that is large enough for crawling, toddling and toys.*

**Plan an eat-in kitchen.** *Wide granite counter doubles as a table for four, great meals or snacks. The U-shaped layout simplifies serving and cleanup.*

**Plan for family activities.** *Families may cook together, play games or enjoy hobbies in the kitchen. For a successful multipurpose room, plan adequate counter space and efficient storage for non-kitchen items.*

# Focus on a great design

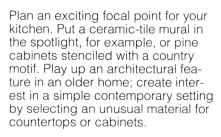

Plan an exciting focal point for your kitchen. Put a ceramic-tile mural in the spotlight, for example, or pine cabinets stenciled with a country motif. Play up an architectural feature in an older home; create interest in a simple contemporary setting by selecting an unusual material for countertops or cabinets.

This bold approach to kitchen design works best if the focal point is planned carefully in terms of scale, shape, color and material. Visualize the kitchen as a complementary setting for the highlighted feature.

**Focus on shape.** *Lively angles define this unusual kitchen. The island and light fixture repeat the shape of the triangular room. The practical benefit: space is used efficiently.*

**Focus on a fireplace.** *Floor-to-ceiling fireplace is the centerpiece of this contemporary kitchen. Details like a raised hearth, brick firebox, simple mantel and gleaming lamps enhance its appeal.*

**Focus on architecture.** Elegant Palladian window opens up a small kitchen by visually expanding the narrow back wall. The graceful lines of the window echo the rich detailing of the traditional cabinets.

**Focus on period style.** Art Deco flowers grow on arched cabinets. The floral design in glass, which is executed in tints popular during the Deco period, defines the color scheme of the kitchen.

# Express your personal style

When you coordinate furnishings, accessories, colors and materials for any room, you express personal style. This individual look usually is compatible with a classic style, such as stately traditional, lively country, sleek and simple contemporary or "inspirational," an eclectic mix of styles.

Study the elements of classic styles through design books, store displays, design seminars and in consultations with kitchen planners. This step refines planning skills, especially for those who are tackling a kitchen design project for the first time. Then confidently express your personal style.

**Contemporary elegance.** *Clean lines, neutral or bold colors and simple accents. European-style cabinets characterize the contemporary look. Other popular features include dramatic high-gloss finishes, low-profile appliances and the latest in counter materials.*

Photo courtesy of Dura Supreme

**Traditional updated.** *Rich wood cabinets are the focus of a traditional kitchen. Look for fine details such as glass doors, pantry storage, decorative molding and high-quality cabinet pulls. Blends well with contemporary colors and materials.*

**Inspirational mix.** *Country/contemporary. Stark white kitchen is warmed with a wood ceiling, rustic antique dining table and American collectibles.*

**Country Accent.** *There's no mistaking this lively style. Rustic cabinets, beamed ceiling and rough-hewn posts echo the interior of a rural cabin. Homespun accessories such as baskets, crocks, and willow furniture set the mood. Contemporary-style appliances keep a low profile.*

Photo courtesy of Merillat Industries

# Color

## Pulls a room together

A strong color scheme gives a kitchen character and unifies the design. Consider a monochromatic plan, in which one color, or shades of one color, dominates. Use this color on large areas, such as cabinets, counters or walls.

Set a mood with color. Dark tones bring walls inward, creating intimate space; whites and neutrals open up a room. Warm up a north-facing kitchen with reds, yellows, oranges. Cool a warm-climate kitchen with white, blues, greens.

◄ ***Warm*** *peach walls glow under the recessed lighting. Oak cabinets take on a light wash of color from the warm walls. Soft green, a color complementary to peach, is a subtle accent.*

Photo courtesy of EXPRESSIONS, A Kitchen & Bath Studio; designed by Lynn Wallace Kelsey

***Pastels.*** *Powdery blue-green furnishings set among neutral counters, walls and cabinets create a serene mood. The white ceiling and the wallcovering reflect light, adding a sunny, fresh feel to the room.*

**Cool,** deep blue and dark-finish traditional cabinets set a formal tone. The kitchen is saved from being too dark and sedate by the light-colored flooring and lively geometric wallcovering.

**Brights.** Intense blue packs a lot of color-power in this bold, contemporary kitchen. The blue laminate cabinets are softened with oak trim and light-colored walls and counters. Select dominant colors carefully, since they often will set the tone for adjoining rooms.

# Creates visual impact

Photo courtesy of Armstrong World Industries, Inc.

For visual impact, use bold splashes of accent color. Intense hues, used judiciously, will heighten the contrast in a color scheme.

Lively accent colors prevent neutral color schemes from becoming too subdued. Areas of strong color may also create eye-catching details in a room that lacks architectural interest.

*Bright yellow* laminate counters accent this kitchen and dining area. Black and white in solids and patterns are an effective mix. Yellow dishes set on white tables create a vibrant contrast.

Photo courtesy of KraftMaid Cabinetry, Inc.

*Brilliant red* accents are all curves, adding interest to the simple lines of cabinets, counters and wallcovering. Graceful hanging lamp, round vase and framed poster create a focal point at the table.

**French blue** knobs, tambour doors, counter edges and molding give a country look to traditional raised-panel cabinets. Patterns make strong accents, too. Note the plaid wallcovering, bordered with blue molding.

Photo courtesy of National Kitchen & Bath Association

**Skylights/spotlights.** *Two generous skylights allow the sun to flood the U-shaped kitchen. Spotlights on a track high in the vault provide general lighting. A second track brightens the cooktop area and turns a dramatic shine on counter and cabinets.*

# Lighting

## Bright looks for cooking and dining

An effective lighting plan combines *general lighting* with *task lighting*. Examples of general lighting include track lights and recessed ceiling fixtures. Working at the sink, cooktop or counter requires task lighting, such as an under-cabinet fixture.

Natural lighting also is an important part of any kitchen plan. Skylights and openings high in the wall, such as clerestory or greenhouse windows, are superior sources of natural light.

Decorative *accent lighting* is taking a more prominent place in kitchen design. A popular choice: lighted glass-front cabinets.

Photo courtesy of WILSONART

**Curved greenhouse** *windows span the work stations in an efficient galley kitchen. Cans mounted on a track (not visible) provide general lighting.*

**Clerestory windows** admit volumes of daylight into this cheerful kitchen. Soft yellow walls reflect the natural light. Attractive accent: lighted cabinet shows off floral china.

**Elegant French doors** topped by an arched window flood this kitchen with natural light. Centrally located fluorescent fixture with diffusing panel provides plenty of general lighting.

**Recessed lights** illuminate the island and create glimmering reflections in the hanging cookware. Under-cabinet task lights brighten the countertops and showcase a plate collection.

**Adjustable lamp** *can be set at the proper height for those who prefer to be seated as they work. Pull the cord, and the lamp rises for those who like to stand while working.*

**Hanging lamps,** *a decorative alternative to cans or track lights, illuminate the cooktop and chopping board. Above the cabinets, indirect lighting fixtures bounce light from the ceiling onto fresh greenery.*

**Trio of lights** *turns the sink area into the focal point of this kitchen. Antique leaded glass windows are flanked by lighted glass-front cabinets. A pair of contemporary recessed lights brightens the counter.* ▶

**Eyeball fixtures,** *spaced to shine on the sink, cooktop and the walkway to the refrigerator, provide even lighting. Dramatic accent: glass blocks, lighted from inside the counter, shimmer with swirling patterns of icy light.*

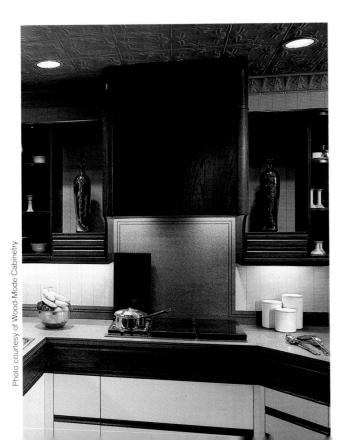

**Custom lighting.** *Fluorescent fixture duplicates the shape of the counter, illuminating a corner sink and two food preparation areas. In its base, opaque glass panels diffuse light. Natural oak frame matches the country-style cabinets.*

◀ **Recessed cans/under-cabinet fixtures.** *Concealed lighting under wall cabinets brightens every square inch of the counters. Recessed cans highlight the cherry display cabinets and range hood.*

Photo courtesy of Lehman & Jones Kitchen Studio; photographed by Mike Krivit

**Wood.** *The top choice for cabinets. Oak, maple, cherry and pine are favorites. Dark woods have a formal, traditional look. Mix woods, too: dark, rich cherry cabinets are set off by light maple flooring.*

Photo courtesy of Wood-Mode Cabinetry

# Materials

## The building blocks of personal style

Simplify the process of selecting materials for your kitchen by shopping for one or two basics at a time. Tackle counters or cabinets first. Flooring and wallcovering may come next.

Cabinet shopping, for example, boils down to two basic choices: wood or laminate. Survey cabinet styles, then select your material. Next, define the details, such as door style, finish or color, trim and storage components.

Flooring, wallcovering and counters offer a diverse range of choices. Some of the more contemporary materials include glass block, marble, granite or hand-painted tile.

Photo courtesy of Wood-Mode Cabinetry

**Light wood.** *Light and natural is the contemporary style in cabinets. Oak cabinets in this monochromatic kitchen are treated with a wash of white stain, minimizing the strong grain pattern.*

◄ **Wood trim.** *Enhance fine wood cabinets with wood pulls and counter trim. Match cabinets and trim, like those in the oak kitchen above, or select contrasting stains or woods for a custom look.*

**Solid-surface material.** *Man-made sheets, up to ¾ inch thick, rival the good looks of granite and marble. Sheets may be cut and shaped like wood. It is an expensive product, but it is durable and resists stains and burns.*

**Laminates.** *Flexible laminate sheets bonded to a substrate, usually particle board, make durable counters and cabinets. An array of dazzling colors and patterns is on the market. Above, dramatic high-gloss black laminate is bonded to curved cabinets.*

**Vinyl flooring.** *Today's sheet vinyls are available in such a huge variety of colors and patterns, they often set the tone for a kitchen's decor. You may want to choose your flooring first, then select complementary counters, cabinets and wallcoverings.* ▶

Photo courtesy of Armstrong World Industries, Inc.

**Glass block,** *once a utilitarian material for basement and bathroom windows, now has a place in high-tech interiors. Glass block transmits light, creates stunning visual patterns and is suitable for structural uses such as the counter base shown above.*

Photo courtesy of WILSONART

**Ceramic tile** *laid in a bold geometric pattern borders an attractive island. Mix tile sizes and colors to create unusual, lively patterns.*

Photo courtesy of Interplan Design Corp.; photographed by DOMIN

Photo courtesy of WILSONART

**Granite-textured laminate** *is cut into strips and applied to curved sliding door. Custom cabinets like this add eye-catching detail.*

**Marble** *is a great material for high-profile areas such as this wet bar. It will withstand a lot of wear and tear while maintaining its beauty.*

**Ceramic tile.** *Customize counters at a moderate cost with patterned tile, tile borders or designs created from tiles of different sizes and colors. Grout colored to match the tile is easier to clean than white grout. Above, earthy tile with floral insets creates a warm kitchen.*

**Marble tile** *in high-gloss black with a fine, white grain makes the island the centerpiece of this two-tone kitchen. Marble is a material that complements both traditional and contemporary decors.*

# Storage Ideas

Storage systems in wood, metal or plastic are optional accessories in most cabinet lines. Select storage components that fit your budget and cooking style, then follow these storage principles: (1) Store items at the point of use. For example, locate pots and pans in drawers or on heavy-duty pull-out shelves near the cooktop. (2) Fit storage to the items stored, such as divided cutlery trays for silverware. (3) Use every cubic inch of storage space. Don't waste space between shelves. The kitchen on page 26 includes excellent storage ideas, which are illustrated in the photos below.

**Pull-out trays** *store cleaning supplies, brushes and nonrefrigerated vegetables in sink base.* **Tilt-down sink panel** *turns wasted space into a storage area for pads, sponges and other supplies used at the sink.*

**Linen trays.** *Shallow sliding trays store linens without wrinkling the fabric. Ideal for tablecloths, placemats and cloth napkins.*

Photos pgs. 26-27 courtesy of Lehman & Jones Kitchen Studio, photographed by Mike Krivit

**Swing-up shelf** *is an ideal way to store less frequently used appliances, like this large mixer.*

**Spice pantry and drawer.** *Island storage puts spices and cooking ingredients within reach of the cooktop. Spice pantry is a fine example of sizing storage to the containers stored. The pull-out drawer allows full use of a deep cabinet.*

# Storage Ideas

**Roll-out serving cart** *glides out from under counter. The three-tier cart is hidden by a false cabinet door when stored. A space-saving accessory for entertaining.*

Photo courtesy of Wood-Mode Cabinetry

**Roll-out table** *is a big asset for small kitchens. It doubles as a counter or a table for two. Its lower work surface is ideal for pastry preparation. For storage, the hinged false drawer in the counter is lifted and the tabletop slides in; the table legs fit in recesses flanking the base cabinet.*

Photo courtesy of Wood-Mode Cabinetry

**Bread drawer,** *a fixture in kitchens in the days before preservatives, is lined with metal and ventilated to keep bread fresh. Pair a bread drawer with a cutting board to create a handy sandwich bar.*

**Corner cabinet trays** *rotate, bringing a collection of crockery into view. The wedge-shaped trays fit exactly on the shelves.*

**Round cabinet/sliding doors.** *Behind tambour-style doors are curved shelves for pots and pans, which are stored directly below the cooktop.*

**Round cabinet/hinged doors.** *Ultra-contemporary island features curved laminate doors with European-style concealed hinges.*

**Pull-out appliance drawer** *frees valuable counter space. Full-extension slides ensure proper support for heavier appliances.*

**Appliance garage.** *Handsome trio of appliance garages with brass tambour doors saves on counter workspace. Two storage nooks hold coffee-making equipment, while a pull-out swivel shelf houses a portable TV.*

**Multilevel storage.** *Pantry with adjustable metal storage baskets is a cook's dream. Every can and package is visible. The tall storage racks in the lower section of the pantry rotate so the shelving behind is easily accessible.*

**Pull-out pantry** *fits neatly into a corner, flush with the laminate desk. Plastic-coated metal storage baskets hung on hooks provide flexible storage.*

*Photo courtesy of Wood-Mode Cabinetry*

**Island pantry** *is a wood variation of the multilevel storage system. Two door racks and the rotating racks inside have space-expanding adjustable shelves. A bonus: narrow shelves at the back of the cabinet are adjustable too.*

*Photo courtesy of WILSONART*

**Pull-out table** *topped with a cutting board is part of a complete baking center. In the upper cabinet are baking supplies, utensil racks, and a mixer plugged in and ready to use. Below the table, attractive wood drawers hold bake ware.*

*Photo courtesy of Cystal Cabinet Works, Inc.*

**Wood pantry,** *which is more expensive than most basket storage systems, is a top choice for kitchens with fine wood cabinets. This pantry features a semicircular lazy Susan in the upper cabinet, with adjustable shelves and rotating racks below.*

Photo courtesy of Armstrong World Industries, Inc.

**Side-by-side ranges,** *shown above, are ideal for large families or for households with more than one cook. Always consider your family's life-style when shopping for appliances and fixtures.*

# Appliances & fixtures

Today's appliances offer features to fit every life-style. Cooktops with inserts for grills, griddles, deep fryers and rotisseries are available; refrigerator/freezers come in dozens of sizes and configurations; stainless steel and ceramic sinks have one, two or three basins, along with numerous styles of faucets, sprayers and other attachments. Down-sized appliances for small kitchens also are available.

Photo courtesy of WILSONART

**Gourmet island.** *A budding gourmet can take cooking lessons at this TV/VCR center. With the swiveling TV, the cook can follow recipe directions, in sequence, as he or she moves to work stations around the island. Details: black octagon sink, built-in wine rack, cookbook shelves, multiple storage drawers.* ▶

**Custom accessories** *turn an ordinary kitchen sink into a convenient work center. Cutting board insert, colander and mini drain board are just some of the options available.*

**Roll-out trash bin** *with pop-up lid is concealed within a drawer that matches the cabinets.*

**Wine cooler** *is a component of a beverage serving center.* ▶
*Other mini-refrigerators are designed for installation in island and base cabinets.*

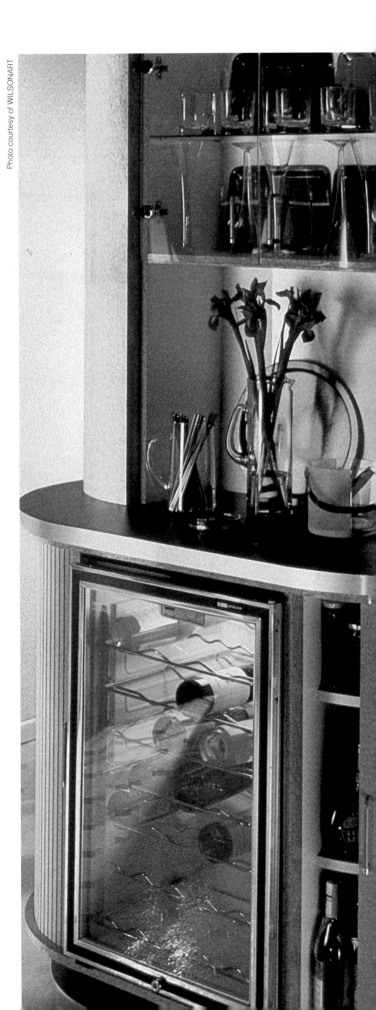

Photo courtesy of Wood-Mode Cabinetry

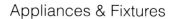

**Graceful sink** is extra deep for preparing flower arrangements or caring for houseplants. Other uses: beverage service center for a party or a children's water fountain.

◄ **Commercial-style range** has four high-temperature gas burners, a griddle and a large oven. Textured range hood hides lights and powerful exhaust fans.

**Corner sink** *expands design possibilities for the small kitchen. The deep, single-bowl sink is located where it is most useful: between the dishwasher and the food preparation counter. An ideal fixture for a one-cook kitchen.*

**Microwave/vent hood.** *Multipurpose microwave has cooktop task lights and vents in its base. A low-profile vent hood for contemporary kitchens.*

**Built-in refrigerator** *fits neatly into a custom cabinet with overhead storage. Bonus: wooden panels on refrigerator door match the rustic cabinetry.* ▶

# A Portfolio of Kitchen Ideas

# Elegant
# TRADITIONAL
## Designs

The traditional kitchen is a showplace for finely crafted wood cabinetry. Oak, walnut and cherry are sought for their distinctive grain. The most popular door styling pairs the cathedral arch wall cabinet with the raised-panel base cabinet. Features like deep crown molding, roomy pantries, open shelving, appliances customized with wood front panels and glass cabinets are hall-marks of traditional styling. Accent with gleaming brass and copper accessories.

**Distinctive double-arch cabinets** *dress up this cottage kitchen. Arched ceiling moldings repeat the cabinet pattern. Space-expanding details; salmon and eggshell color scheme, drop-leaf rolling table stored under counter, and floor-to-ceiling cabinets.*

◄ **Light oak cabinets** *blend with the almond laminate counters and ceramic tile floor. Oak is crafted into the counter edge, dishwasher front, appliance garage and distinctive ceiling. Extras like the center island, bar sink, low pastry counter and built-in computer desk reflect this family's life-style.*

# Details that define the style

▼ **Two-tier china cabinet** is a stunning display case for fine tableware. Curved side panels and inset base reduce its bulk. Traditional accents: leaded glass doors and brass cabinet pulls.

▼ **Cooktop and grill** are set into an opening that resembles a fireplace hearth. Floral ceramic tile unites the island with the cooking area. Pantry is topped with deep molding and dentil.

▲ **Plate rail** spans two walls above the oak cabinetry. Along its base are task lights. Brass chandelier with replicas of oil lamps is another traditional touch.

▼ **Oversize Palladian window** with rich wood trim is the focal point of this U-shaped kitchen. It transforms an ordinary, narrow kitchen into an extraordinary room.

Photo courtesy of KraftMaid Cabinetry, Inc.

**Oak range hood,** which matches the cabinetry in this kitchen, is a handsome way to conceal ventilation fans over the European-style cooktop. Oak spice rack and open shelving have a custom-made appearance.

Photo courtesy of Quaker Maid, div. WCI, Inc.

**Oversize range hood** combines traditional oak with the clean, simple lines of contemporary styling.

Photo courtesy of Wood-Mode Cabinetry

**Crown molding** and a ceiling fan/light fixture add an old-time flavor to this traditional yet very up-to-date kitchen. The roomy kitchen is well suited to the dark cabinets with arched-panel doors and earthy ceramic tile walls and counters.

*Large island* with durable laminate countertop doubles the amount of space for food preparation. The sink, stove and pantry are within easy reach. Rounded countertop corners and inset double-cabinet base visually reduce its size.

# Islands that fit your life-style

Kitchens of the last century were dominated by a large, central work table. Today, the kitchen island replaces that old-fashioned table. An island expands counter space, increases storage capacity and provides an area for casual dining. Drop in a cooktop with downdraft ventilation, plumb a second sink or wire an electric outlet in the island. For entertaining, invite guests to sit at the island while dinner is prepared.

*Cooktop island* is a snack bar, too. Base ▶ cabinets accommodate downdraft ventilation equipment and two storage cabinets. Stools tuck neatly under the almond laminate countertop trimmed with wood. Angled side aids traffic flow around the island.

**Brilliant blue laminate** unites the island with the counter behind it. There's plenty of space to set pots, pans, and cooking utensils on either side of the island cooktop. Chop ingredients at the butcher block counter, then mix and cook at the island. Stools are out of the way, protected by side panels.

*A contemporary black-and-white color scheme* can work in a traditional kitchen. The trick: use more white than black. Here, handsome black counters and island are balanced with white cabinetry and a sweeping window. Aqua and rattan stools add warm texture and color to the two-tone kitchen.

## TRADITIONAL

# Bright looks for elegant designs

Crisp, fresh white gives traditional cabinets a contemporary look. The durable painted surfaces wipe clean easily. A little bit of color goes a long way in an all-white kitchen. Touches like a ceramic tile backsplash, bright cabinet pulls or antique china displayed behind glass doors are strong accents. A must with white cabinetry: white appliances.

*Yellow and blue wallcovering* with strong diagonal pattern makes a sunny background for white cabinetry. Deep blue solid-surface countertops blend with the wallcovering. Glass cabinets display a colorful collection of china. White double oven, refrigerator and dishwasher complete the look.

*Tiny telephone nook* is big on color. Bright aqua cushions accent the black-and-white scheme (see photo, far left). Color details count: notice the cushion piping, striped wallcovering and wall lamp. Overhead cabinets and bench drawers in this charming corner expand storage space.

Photo courtesy of Crystal Cabinet Works, Inc.

Photo courtesy of KitchenAid, Inc.

# Cabinets go light and natural

A new chapter in kitchen design began when traditional cabinets were manufactured with light or natural finishes. Cabinet construction has been updated, too. Many styles are frameless, so doors and drawers fit flush; no cabinet frame is visible. The cabinetry blends beautifully with contemporary patterns and colors in wallcovering, flooring and window treatments.

Photo courtesy of KraftMaid Cabinetry, Inc.

Photo courtesy of Crystal Cabinet Works, Inc.

***The most efficient floor plan:*** *an L-shaped kitchen with island. The refrigerator, sink and cooktop are within easy reach. The solid-surface counters and white ceramic tile island lighten the room. Wood panels camouflage the refrigerator and dishwasher.*

◄ ***Light oak frameless cabinets*** *are pared down to essentials. Gracefully arched window and cooking enclosure complement the straight-line cabinetry. The simple pantry and copper cookware pick up the traditional theme. A space saver: snack bar set below counter height replaces the kitchen table.*

**Entertain beautifully** *in an elegant kitchen/dining area with matching cabinetry. Oak buffet contains bar sink, glass storage and wine rack for beverage service. Curved kitchen peninsula topped with granite-pattern laminate is convenient for serving and clearing the table. Soft gray wallcovering and flooring unite the area.*

TRADITIONAL

# Dressed for entertaining

**Distinctive textures** make this small kitchen ▶ a standout. Ceramic tile on walls, counters and floor is mixed with oak cabinets and granite-look laminate table. Traditional details: glass china cabinet, spice boxes and a pantry.

▼ **Dress up** raised-panel cabinets with molding, flush doors and brass pulls. The rounded edge on laminate counters and above cabinets softens the look. Details like open shelves, a raised serving bar and double ceramic sink with high-rise faucet express personal style.

Photo courtesy of Dura Supreme

Photo opposite page courtesy of KraftMaid Cabinetry, Inc.

Photo courtesy of KraftMaid Cabinetry, Inc.

# Charming Country Kitchens

Country means comfort, great food, good company. The country kitchen is a relaxed, informal room that combines modern convenience with easygoing charm. Define the style with naturals like pine cabinets, plank flooring, willow baskets and stoneware. Fill your country haven with heirloom quilts and handcarved furnishings or an exuberant display of collectibles. Country mixes well with almost any style, from Victorian to contemporary, so it's easy to modify the look of your home.

Photos pages 52 and 53 courtesy of Armstrong World Industries, Inc.

**Hefty beams and posts** set a country mood. Rustic cabinets with wrought-iron hinges conceal the refrigerator and provide storage. An antique woodstove shares kitchen duty with a modern cooktop. Overhead, a lively collection of baskets and cookware.

**Country great room** spans two stories. The open, airy space easily accommodates a large ▶ pine refectory table and comfortable Windsor chairs. A collection of American folk art personalizes the cheerful dining area.

***Updated country kitchen*** *combines tile counters and rich oak cabinets with massive beams and vintage kitchenalia. Flavor the mix of old and new with whitewashed walls and a cooktop set into a curved alcove.*

Photo courtesy of Wood-Mode Cabinetry

**Open shelving** extended to the ceiling holds a whimsical mix of kitchen gadgets. Pine cabinets stocked with glassware and serving pieces flank the sink.

Photo courtesy of Wood-Mode Cabinetry

**Hearty country cooking** requires pots and pans in abundance. A handsome display of gleaming cookware hangs from butcher hooks on a sturdy pot rack above the island. Plate rack shows off Colonial-era pewter dishes.

# Details define country style. Three ways to get just the right look

◀ ***Use natural materials.*** *Woods like pine, light oak and maple go with the country style. Antique maple butcher block is an all-purpose workspace. Sturdy butcher-block counters are set on primitive cabinets. A wooden paddle fan blends with the pine ceiling.*

***Make a color statement.*** *An eye-catching tile backsplash in warm browns and gray-blue is painted with country designs. Blue molding on the crisp white French-style cabinetry unites the color scheme.* ▶

***Reproduce a handcrafted design.*** *Tile patterns resemble stenciling, a decorating technique popular in the 18th and 19th centuries. A stylized vine surrounds the pass-through window. Farm animals decorate the tile walls.* ▶

# Create your own theme

**Fresh country.** It's always spring in this pastel-and-white kitchen. Flowers bloom on the contemporary-style wallcovering. A tile border of pale blue garlands accents the counters and walls. High-quality oak cabinets with brass pulls and a pair of rush-seat chairs embellished with flowers set a formal tone.

◄ **Barnyard geese** wearing floral collars look right at home by the bay window. Large-scale accessories like these life-size animals enhance a theme kitchen.

**Leaded glass cabinets,** brass candlesticks and the sophisticated table setting are worthy of a dining room, yet they fit into this simple, elegant kitchen. Unique range hood unites three design elements: fresh white, blue tile and fine wood.

**Whimsical rabbits,** a traditional symbol of spring, sniff fresh fruit on the counter. A few well-chosen accessories can be as eye-catching as a cluster of small-scale objects. ►

All photos pages 58 and 59 courtesy of Kitchens & Baths by Design; David Skomsvold, designer; Ed Cox, Michael Raabe, contractors

# Relaxed dining

Why not dine in your country kitchen, close to the aromas of good cooking? Basic ingredients: a generous table and wide, comfortable chairs. Keep the service informal, and add fresh or dried flowers to the table.

Photo courtesy of Armstrong World Industries, Inc.

Photo courtesy of Wood-Mode Cabinetry

*Garden kitchen* full of windows and plants makes country dining a pleasure. Honey oak table and Windsor chairs match the finely crafted cabinetry Earthy tile floor warms the neutral color scheme.

◄ *Graceful pine table* and cushioned chairs welcome diners to a country gourmet kitchen. The cooking alcove with its striking wood surround holds a double cooktop and side-by-side ovens. A great place to cook a garden harvest feast.

*Touches of blue* and open shelves dominate this understated kitchen. Creamy white cabinets with a low-gloss finish have a subtle shine. Paned glass and scalloped cabinet trim further define the French country look.

Country

_____

# Add a French accent. Mix fresh white, strong blue and gaily colored flowers

**Stunning floral mural** grows across the center island. Collector plates repeat the floral theme. White finish on the oak cabinets minimizes the strong grain pattern. ▶

**Fresh-cut wildflowers,** *captured in tile, decorate the range hood and wall. Bands of blue enhance the floral pastels. The textured hood surface resembles the whitewashed walls found in traditional French country homes.*

Country

**Victorian influence.** *Dark cabinets embellished with dentil molding and lattice cuts are teamed with a handsome parquet floor. Deep-red laminate counters match the striped wallcovering. Classic plaid country curtains dress the tall, narrow windows.*

# Classic patterns: plaids and small prints

Photo courtesy of Dura Supreme

***Country-modern*** *kitchen unites contemporary colors and classic cabinetry. Two-color laminate counters and a checkerboard floor dominate the room. Wallcovering and curtain fabric in small-scale patterns coordinate with the colorful accessories.*

***Open shelving*** *stocked with provisions in see-through containers makes a kitchen feel country. Redware and serving dishes are on display in glass cabinets.* ▶

Photo courtesy of Wood-Mode Cabinetry

# Stunning
# CONTEMPORARY
## Designs

Streamlined describes the clean, crisp, contemporary look. The recipe: mix a *minimum* of materials and patterns for *maximum* effect. Sleek European-style cabinets with overlay doors are the top choice for this style. Sophisticated looks combine curving shapes, dramatic color schemes and high-gloss finishes. Color favorites: white and neutrals.

Photo courtesy of Interplan Design Corp. photographed by DOMIN

**Basic black** *polished-granite counters teamed with gray laminate cabinets create a dramatic two-color kitchen. Eye-catching angles: triangular dining counter complements cabinets rising across the wall.*

◄ **Basic white** *laminate cabinets set the stage for bright accessories. Strong black-and-white floorcovering pattern is in scale with the oversize island. Marble-look wallcovering softens a wall of cabinetry.*

Photo courtesy of Dura Supreme

# CONTEMPORARY

**Small kitchen** has handsome tan cabinets that fade into cream walls, visually expanding the room. Streamlined space-savers: appliance garage, built-in refrigerator, and microwave with vent and lights in base.

**Soaring wall** neatly frames the kitchen. ▶ Curved counter and simple stools invite guests to perch. An unusual use of pastels in a contemporary kitchen.

◀ **Icy glass** contrasts with warm peach walls and cabinets in this spacious kitchen/living area. Rounded bilevel counter, chrome stools and cone lights modify the straight-line look.

# Color scheming

Cabinet and counter colors dominate a kitchen, but there are no hard-and-fast rules about *which* color goes *where*. These kitchens demonstrate very different solutions to dual-color design.

***Clean white, warm brown.*** *White soffits visually extend cabinets to the ceiling. Granite counters provide texture and color. Ultramodern shine: mirrored backsplash, chrome canisters, stainless-steel double sink.*

***High-gloss black, soft gray.*** *Cabinets combine color, shine and curves to create storage as interesting as sculpture. Textured granite counters contrast with the glossy cabinets.* ▶

# White: pure and simple

White sets the stage. Touches of color, texture and pattern stand out against white cabinets, walls and counters. Complementary elements: white appliances, warm lighting, colorful accents.

Photo courtesy of Interplan Design Corp.; photographed by DOMIN

Photo courtesy of Merillat Industries

**Pure white** *shows off the colors of food and flowers. A great kitchen to personalize with accessories in bold colors.*

**Focal Point.** *Gleaming copper and brass hood is the centerpiece of this kitchen, set off by white raised-panel cabinets, white counter and floor. Brass rails and cabinet pulls shine under recessed lights.*

# CONTEMPORARY

**Subtle textures** *of the light gray flooring, counters and wallcovering become important in the minimal kitchen. Another strong element: wide vertical trim that punctuates the wall and base cabinets.*

▶

**White and gray.** *This unusual design pairs white wall cabinets with soft gray base units. Creamy white solid-surface counter unifies the mix. Tableware displayed on open shelves adds subtle color.*

**Blue-gray trim** *forms a horizontal pattern on simple white cabinets in this small kitchen. Shallow cabinets above the sink increase storage without projecting into the work area.*

# High-style wood

Select wood cabinetry for a warm contemporary look. Sleek European cabinets are available in a variety of hardwoods and stained finishes. Consider other uses of wood: on butcher-block counters, for cabinet trim and pulls, on light fixtures, around windows and doors.

**Combine wood and laminate**. *Wood trim on laminate cabinets stands out in this gray and rose kitchen. Matching wood dresses up the appliance garage, bay window frame and lighting fixture over the island.*

**All-wood cabinets.** *European cabinets with vertical and horizontal planks are a distinctive alternative to laminate cabinets. Soft-blue tile counter and floral backsplash create the cheerful look of spring.* ▶

# CONTEMPORARY

◀ ***A bold mix*** *of rosewood and laminate creates a light, contemporary cabinet in spite of the dark stain. Rosewood crafted in the window frame, cabinet pulls, corner shelving and plank ceiling unify the design.*

***Contemporary curves*** *dominate the wood-and-laminate storage wall and multilevel counter. Simple flooring and wallcovering form a neutral background for the high-contrast cabinet materials.*

***Patio door, skylight and window*** *bathe kitchen in natural light. Supplements to natural lighting: recessed fixtures over island, task lights over sink and cooktop, track lights for general illumination.*

# In the right light

CONTEMPORARY

Photo opposite page courtesy of Quaker Maid, div. WCI, Inc.

Photo courtesy of Crystal Cabinet Works, Inc.

Photo courtesy of Armstrong World Industries, Inc.

**Balanced light.** *Patio door plus window at opposite end of kitchen let the sun in throughout the day. White laminate cabinets and natural light enlarge the small space.*

◄ **Window wall** *casts a warm glow over the sink and counters. Flooring and wallcoverings in shades of rust add to the feeling of warmth, which is balanced by light-colored cabinets and counters.*

*Circles and curves* dominate this gray and black kitchen. Multilevel island with vertical laminate is the focal point. Storage wall on the left and cabinetry on right were custom-made for the curved floor plan.

# Clever curves, smart storage

*Spice racks* recessed into wall below granite-patterned cabinets are close to the mixing area. Detail: sculpted recess in solid-surface panel holds fresh flowers. ▶

**Recessed appliance garages** *store coffee-maker, juicer and coffee grinder. Custom-crafted nooks such as these keep counters uncluttered while providing easy access to appliances.*

**Sliding door** *reveals table linen and silverware storage at the island eating area. Circular cupboard could contain almost any tableware needed for meals.*

▶

**Microwave shelf** *provides a space-saving counter for food and dishes. It slides out of the way when not in use.*

◀ **Lighted glass cabinet** *houses a collection of delicate sea creatures. Recessed fixtures illuminate the interior shelves. More curves: desk and cabinet side panels.*

# Exciting
# *INSPIRATIONAL*
## *Kitchens*

The most exciting kitchens are a dynamic blend of *classic style* and *personal style*. So go ahead and mix, whether your taste is traditional, country or contemporary. Find inspiration at home in a treasured antique, a bright poster, travel souvenirs or grandmother's floral china. Here are a dozen stunning kitchens to get you started.

**Regional style.** *Southwestern galley kitchen tucked behind adobe fireplace mixes sleek European cabinets with rustic counters. Regional elements: rough ceiling beams, carved stool and plank shelving lined with copper cookware, baskets and earthy pottery.*

◄ **Best of the Southwest.** *Muted desert colors and Spanish-style whitewashed walls connect the living room and kitchen. Native Southwestern materials are abundant, such as leather chair, animal hide rug, handwoven blankets, steer horns and terra-cotta accessories.*

# Borrow from the past

Capture an era with colors, patterns and furnishings from the past. For example, mimic a fifties kitchen, emphasizing chrome, metal cabinets and colors like aqua/black/white. Or, create a Victorian room with a palette of deep jewel tones and cabinets rich in decorative detail.

◄ **Art Deco kitchen** *has the bold outlines and streamlined look popular in the twenties and thirties. Deep green trims the pastel base cabinets and peach counters. Focal point: arched cabinets with graceful flowers.*

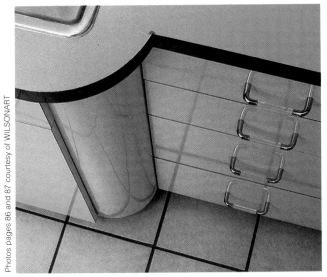

Photos pages 86 and 87 courtesy of WILSONART

**Curved panel** *joins sink cabinet and contemporary-style drawers. Art Deco designers experimented with new materials, like plastics. These high-gloss laminate cabinets and chrome-and-plastic drawer pulls are reminiscent of that tradition.*

**Arched glass doors** *extend above the cabinets to create a stunning look for this kitchen (far left). Dark cabinet interiors set off white tableware (above).*

# Classic kitchens with updated styling

◄ **New Orleans-style** *great room is summertime cool in crisp white and sky blue. Garden greenery, lazy fans and louvered shutters define the romantic Southern look. The spice: triangular island that centralizes cooktop, sink, dishwasher and storage.*

Photos pages 88 and 89 courtesy of Armstrong World Industries, Inc.

**Traditional redefined.** *Light, natural finish and European overlay doors update the traditional raised-panel cabinets. More contemporary touches: white and tan tile, whitewashed range hood, pearly solid-surface counters, soaring cathedral ceiling.*

# Strong colors, bold shapes

**Silver stripes** shine against inky black. The steely bands flow across the room, changing from broad to narrow. Custom cabinet doors and appliance fronts are necessary to achieve the unbroken lines. The high-contrast materials and finishes create the dramatic look. ▶

**Square power.** The simple square is given the spotlight in this black and white kitchen. Squares appear in the checkerboard flooring, white ceiling and black ceramic wall tiles.

**White alcove** is set off by black ceramic tiles with red grout. The gentle arch of the alcove contrasts with the squares that dominate the kitchen's design.

Photos pages 90 and 91 courtesy of WILSONART

***Dynamic colors unite three rooms*** *in this open-plan home. Kitchen colors are balanced; no single hue dominates. Black appliances contrast with white cabinets and bright yellow counters. Distinctive details: textured black walls, mini-tables, Oriental-style chairs, sliding doors.*

# Simplicity
# in black

***Purely Oriental.*** *Traditional Japanese screens enclose an intimate dining area with mustard-colored walls. Lacquered dining table, red dishes and Oriental-style chairs enhance the Eastern theme. In the compact kitchen: Black Shoji screen, black cabinetry, black plate rack.*

# American originals

▼ **Spacious kitchen** blends turn-of-the-century charm with contemporary good looks. Old-fashioned details include painted cabinets, graceful hanging lamp, Palladian window and paneled ceiling. Brass range hood is set off by diamond-pattern ceramic wall tile.

**Collector's kitchen** mixes 19th and 20th century design. Crisp white European cabinets are topped with a display of Americana. Antique pine refectory table complements the country hutch displaying heirloom china. The butcher-block island counter, pine cathedral ceiling and bleached flooring warm the white walls and cabinetry.

# Bare minimum: when less is more

**Neutrals** *create a serene kitchen. Understated palette includes oyster island and cabinets, sandy ceramic tile, taupe refrigerator and gray walls. Glass block sparkles and walls turn silver under strategically placed recessed lights.*

◄ **Essentials.** *Ultrasleek kitchen bares its walls and virtually eliminates decoration. The result: contours of the distinctive island and overhead light panel have a big impact. Sink, cooktop, storage and serving bar are housed in the long, curved island. Unusual focal point: stairway silhouette.*

Photos on these pages courtesy of WILSONART

**Bright geometrics.** *Siren-red booth, black restaurant table and round hanging light are arranged symmetrically in front of an asymmetric wall. Bold kitchen colors are intensified against a background of white cabinets, soffit and ceiling washed in warm sunlight.*

▼ **Building blocks.** *Drawers, range and wine cooler line up like matched cubes. Repeated theme: asymmetric backsplash marches to its own tune. Whimsical folk carvings and textiles soften the sharp geometrics.*

# Bathroom Ideas

# What Makes a Great Bathroom?

A great bathroom enables you to take care of your needs in a comfortable, attractive and convenient setting. Whether you are showering or shaving, a great bathroom lets you do so in a relaxed and pleasant fashion. It is a place you can retreat to in privacy, spending uninterrupted time tending to your needs. It reflects you individual sense of style by displaying your love of particular colors, your favorite textures and patterns. To help you plan your perfect bathroom, we have gathered over 150 color photographs of bathroom designs and styles and compiled them in *A Portfolio of Bathroom Ideas*.

This book will set you well on your way to creating a bathroom specifically suited to your taste and needs. First we cover the essentials of planning a great bathroom, such as determining what your needs are compared to your budget and learning how to recognize your own unique style. We then present the design elements for creating a wonderful bathroom: space (large and small), color (bright and dark), lighting (natural and artificial), and materials (marble, ceramic and wood). We show bathroom highlights that cover your choice of interesting appliances, unique fixtures and vanities. Then we elaborate on bathroom themes covering styles from country and romantic to garden and contemporary. Finally, we present pictures of distinctive bathrooms, where we show you unique ways to plan a bathroom theme and how to add to existing features. Whether you are starting from scratch or planning to remodel an existing bath, this book will help you plan a room that will not only meet your needs but will be a place of comfort, pleasure and even inspiration.

Photo courtesy of Kohler Co.

Photo courtesy of American Olean Tile Company

# Planning

## Assessing your needs

When considering bathroom decorating, whether you are thinking of completely remodeling or simply a face-lift, your first step is to determine your needs. Needs have to do with the people your bath will be servicing: how many of them there are and their ages, as well as how often they will be using it.

Are there just two of you, or do you have a large family? Maybe your home includes two working adults, both needing to get off to an early start each morning. Or perhaps your schedules allow you to make use of the same bath at different times during the day. What about children? Infants and young children have needs that are very different from those of the growing teenager. Is there an elderly person living with you, or one who visits often? Special features that make bathrooms convenient and safe for individuals with specific needs and limitations can be incorporated.

Now is also the time to think of future needs, such as career development or planning a new family. Whether or not you will be staying in your home for years to come or want to move in a short time will also affect the type of decorating you'll be undertaking. Considering these aspects of your life will help you develop an image of your ideal bathroom.

Next you need to decide if you will be completely remodeling an existing bath, adding on an entirely new room, or simply redecorating a bathroom that is perfectly functional but in need of cosmetic changes.

Remodeling can be as simple as adding an extra washbasin or extensive enough to involve changing the plumbing in order to accommodate a whirlpool. Redesigning an existing bath generally includes replacing appliances and fixtures without changing the basic structure of the bath; more extensive work makes adding on a new room a more realistic option. Adding on also lets you have the fun of designing your dream bath, making the space exactly the size you want and giving you the chance to include amenities you might not otherwise be able to accommodate.

Another option to consider is the possibility of adding a half bath. These small rooms, including only a toilet and a sink, can alleviate the stress of inadequate bathroom space without involving a large amount of time, effort and money. An empty corner, an extra closet and even unused space under a stairway can be turned into a delightful and functional smaller bathroom.

Careful consideration of all these aspects, from the people in your life to what type of bathroom restructuring you want to undertake, is your first step toward a satisfying bathroom decorating experience.

# Recognizing your style

Bathrooms come in as many styles as people do. Choosing a style that matches your personality is your second step after determining your needs.

What kind of atmosphere do you want this room to convey? Do you want it to be a friendly and welcoming room, or exotic, full of elaborate appliances and unusual odds and ends? This room can be a simple place with a basic color scheme and little ornamentation, or it can be full of fun, making use of bright, bold colors in interesting combinations and patterns. You might want to fill it with antiques, covering the walls with old-fashioned pictures and adding an armoire, or perhaps you would like to decorate all in white, adding just one other color as an accent.

As you consider your personal style and preferences, think of the rest of your house. What types of decorating schemes have you used in other rooms? Do you like them, or are there things about these rooms you would like to change?

Photos on this page courtesy of Kohler Co.

Looking at pictures in magazines or reading home improvement books is a great place to start. Notice which baths leap out at you. You can also visit model homes, noting the decorating schemes professionals have used.

Your style, once you have defined it, will be expressed in a variety of ways. You will be choosing colors and patterns, using materials such as wood or ceramic or stone, and deciding on sources of natural and artificial lighting. Each of these areas is an avenue for personal expression. You might use them in imaginative ways or along more conservative lines. Perhaps you will pick a single theme to repeat throughout the room, or will want to take a more eclectic approach that combines many different techniques.

Whatever you choose, you want your bath to be a place you are comfortable in, a room that is as personal as your wardrobe and as familiar as a friend.

# Determining your budget

Your final consideration, after assessing your needs and deciding upon your style, is your budget. How much money do you have to work with, and where is it coming from? You might wish to undertake a major renovation but only have enough money for a smaller remodeling job. Or perhaps you're willing to invest in an entirely new bath, whether that means building on a whole new room or restructuring an existing one. You will either have worked to save enough money for this new project, will be getting some type of loan or will be limiting yourself to a smaller decorating project that your current budget can handle.

While financing is usually available for home improvement, you should consider the value of your home as well as how long you plan to stay in it before making any final decisions. Adding a $6,000 bath to a home in a neighborhood of moderate incomes doesn't

help the resale value; however, a smaller redecorating job might be just the thing to make it marketable. If you plan to stay in your home, major changes make sense because you will be able to enjoy the added bath for years to come. New appliances are a large investment you might be able to skip if you currently have a newer bath with functioning appliances.

Sticking to adding accessories and changing the wallpaper lets you redecorate without great expense. However, if you are renovating an older home or adding on a bath, you will have to purchase appliances as well as additional features such as windows, mirrors and light fixtures. Whatever route you take, the budget you have to work with is a factor you must consider, along with your current needs and personal preferences. Thinking carefully about all these options before beginning will give you a good start toward creating a great bathroom.

Photo courtesy of Armstrong World Industries, Inc.

# Space

## Size

Physical size is your number one consideration when determining bathroom decorating. How big or little is your bathroom going to be? Bathrooms come in various shapes and sizes, and whether you are creating an entirely new room or redecorating an existing bath will determine in part the options you will be working with.

For many people who are creating a bathroom from scratch, choosing a larger space allows them to develop a room that includes a variety of amenities and extra items a smaller room cannot provide. These can be everything from extra cupboards, drawers and counter space to additional appliances, such as a bidet or a shower stall separate from the tub.

Small baths are captivating, with their own versions of charm and style, and give you the chance to come up with creative uses of space. Interesting features are included in these smaller rooms: tiny windows and mirrors, unusual sinks, modest tables or shelves. In any case, remember that the size of your bath is only the beginning of your decorating experience.

*The peaceful feeling of a private bathing area has been created in this room, although bedroom and bath occupy the same space. Set off from the rest of the room and placed at an angle, the tub occupies definite space that seems like a separate room. French doors leading outside lend a romantic air to the entire room.*

Photo courtesy of Kohler Co.

**Lots of unused floor space,** combined with an all-white ceiling, gives this room a feeling of spaciousness. Appliances that encircle the room leave the middle area open for traffic flow or the addition of extra features, and add to its expansiveness.

**Extra room** is gained in this bathroom by tucking the toilet and bidet behind the shower area. An illusion of space can also be created by leaving the shower stall transparent and continuous with the rest of the bath.

**Additional privacy** is gained in this room by placing the toilet and bidet behind a half wall and down a step. This area, separate from the lavatory and full-length window, is hidden from view and allows the option of accommodating more than one individual at a time.

**A popular feature** in the larger bath is the installation of a shower separate from the tub. This room is set up to include a drying area outside the shower stall where towels, a robe and other clothing can remain dry, yet easily accessible. A glass block "window" between the tub and the shower visually connects this room's double bathing area.

**The effect of two rooms** instead of one has been created here by separating the bathing area from the rest of the bath. This feature is especially helpful when several people make use of the same bath, or it can be chosen simply to allow greater privacy.

# Storage

Storage includes closets, drawers, shelves, cupboards and cubbyholes that can hold accessories, linens and other items needed in the bathroom. Some baths are large enough to offer a variety of storage options. Others have little if any space for storage, making it necessary to utilize every available nook and cranny. Items used for storage can be selected to accentuate your design theme; you also may choose to be creative with objects not ordinarily associated with storage in the bathroom.

**Shelves** staggered next to the toilet allow a small reading area to be set up, while the extensive use of wall space aids in decorating this smaller bathroom.

**This small vanity** includes an assortment of cupboard and drawer spaces in interesting shapes and sizes. Lots of cupboards can be used, not only to store linens and personal accessories, but for any number of other household items.

**With its many cubbyholes,** this rustic cupboard provides a unique answer to the bath without closet space or one simply in need of extra storage. Rolling the towels rather than folding them makes creative use of available space.

# Color

The color of your bathroom plays a close second to its size when making choices about bathroom decorating. You can feature colors that are bright and bold or of a quieter nature, perhaps the softer pastels. You might want to include several shades, using bright red to accent a softer gray, or a misty green and pastel pink against an off-white background.

Don't forget to consider the color schemes of other rooms in your home in order to maintain an overall sense of style. Remember that lighter colors, especially white, can make a room appear larger than it is and are especially helpful in smaller quarters; while darker colors have the effect of making a room look smaller, limiting their use in a small or medium-size bath, but making them an excellent choice for retaining intimacy in a larger room.

Choosing a color scheme also includes considering patterns. You can pick from many varieties of flowers, stripes, squares and other prints. You might choose to decorate with simple designs or along more intricate lines. Or come up with your own combination. Whatever your choice, color is an exciting medium to work with and offers you the chance to express your individuality, using various tones and interesting designs.

*Bright pink and aqua blue* are used extensively in this bath, filling it with color. The floor, tub and sink make use of the same pattern, providing contrast to the quieter gray on the walls.

*Using **bright colors** in a daring pattern on the floor, this room relies on simple stripes and a lighter color on the walls for softness and balance.*

Photo courtesy of Grohe America

**An unusual color combination** of sea green walls in contrast with a red floor and red trim around the mirror is used in this room. The stark white of the sinks and tub are reflected in the mirror and stand out in sharp relief against the heavier tones.

**Fire-engine red,** the sink, blinds and trim in this bathroom catch the eye while bold black tiles and a smaller black-and-white-pattern offer balance. Note the identical trim around the mirror and window; red blinds reflected in the mirror trick the eye into seeing it as another window. Or is the window really a mirror?

Photo courtesy of Color Tile, Inc.

***This striking black lavatory*** *with its pure white bowl is a bold addition to this room. Its strong visual presence creates a focal point that can be commanding on its own or used in combination with other interesting features.*

**White walls** are set off sharply by the deep blue trim in this room. The sink and cabinets underneath become a focal point while blue-and-white towels complete this simple, yet striking, scheme.

**Gray, pink and aqua blue** *combine to give this bathroom a quiet touch and extend an invitation to relax in this peaceful room at the end of a tiring day.*

# Lighting

## Natural and artificial

Lighting is an essential feature in every bathroom. We use both natural and artificial light daily in the various rooms throughout our homes. Windows let in natural light, connecting us to the sun and the world outside.

Natural light comes through windows. These can be just about any shape or size you choose, and can be set in various areas of the bath to create a specific atmosphere or tone. Paned windows are often placed next to or surrounding the tub, creating a bathing area separate from the rest of the room. Windows set above the sink provide extra light that helps with grooming. Uniquely shaped windows can become the room's focal point, apart from other features.

Windows can be customized, their interesting shapes serving a decorative as well as a practical purpose. Skylights provide depth as they let in light from unique

*Large windows* not only let in lots of light, but also create a sense of spaciousness. Here the tub is set apart from the rest of the bath and surrounded with tall paned windows, giving the luxurious impression of an extra room and offering a vista of the world outdoors.

*Lots of light* comes into this room through these two large, angular windows. Because they are set at an angle and are continuous with the lines of the wall, they are an appealing decorating feature as well as a great source of natural light.

and unexpected directions. Soft light sets a romantic tone, while bright lights illuminate dark corners.

Artificial light provides us with the ability to create light whenever we choose, making rooms functional at night. Beyond providing us with the ability to see, lighting can be used to create atmosphere and determine mood. Artificial light is available in different styles such as incandescent, which is very bright and an excellent choice around mirrors, or fluorescent, which is environmentally safe and less expensive.

Don't forget that wherever there is light, shadows appear, which provides intriguing decorating possibilities. Let your sources of natural and artificial light balance each other so that your room can be pleasantly lit any time of the day or night.

**Thick glass blocks** *cover nearly two full walls in this room, providing privacy as they let in light. A popular window choice that is also used as a room divider, glass blocks obscure images but allow ample light to shine through.*

**Three large, round skylights** supply this spacious room with light from above, while glass blocks, mirrors and extra ceiling fixtures

*provide an array of additional lighting possibilities that make each activity area functional and safe.*

Photo courtesy of National Kitchen & Bath Association; project designed by Shelley Patterson, L. Jones

**This room uses light** from a variety of sources and directions. Windows, ceiling lights, fixtures above the mirror and the two lights directly over the bathtub provide a number of lighting options.

**These two lighting examples,** *showing artificial versus natural light, display the differences in tone and mood between the two. Both types of light allow us to see, but artificial light can be used in softer tones to create a subtle effect, while bright natural light provides strong contrast with its shadows.*

**In this room,** *glass blocks are again used for the window treatment. The large window area lets in light that, although diffused, is still bright, while it also provides privacy. The interesting shape and texture of glass block makes it an excellent decorating feature.*

# Accoutrements

Lighting accoutrements are items such as mirrors and bathroom accents that combine with existing sources of light to provide additional illumination. They are used to enhance existing sources of light, but also serve as decorating features in themselves.

***Beautifully arched*** *and conveniently placed above the sink and counter area, this mirror reflects the rest of the bath in its smooth surface. Its unique shape gives an added dimension of elegance to this bath.*

**Bright light** fills the eye in this all-white room, pouring in through the window and bouncing off the mirror and other reflective surfaces. Accents such as gold fixtures and yellow flowers provide warmth and depth, almost as if they were sources of light themselves.

**Stained glass** *can be used for a unique lighting option, adding interesting color and pattern to the room. These ornate windows are decorated with bright flowers and intertwining vines. Available in a variety of designs, stained glass can also be made to order, letting you choose your own colors and patterns.*

Photos courtesy of Stained Glass Overlay of St. Paul / Minneapolis

***Colorful light*** *spills into this room through two stained-glass windows made up of simple rectangles. Brilliant reds, yellows and blues spread over the floor, reflecting off the wall and the white appliances and filling the room with their warm hues.*

# Materials

The materials you choose for your bath will be used to cover not only the walls and floor, but your appliances as well. You have the option of using a variety of materials, such as combining wooden cabinets and floors with ceramic tiles and porcelain appliances. Many other options are available, however, like stone, plastic laminates and vinyl flooring; your choice of material will help determine the atmosphere of the room and convey your bathroom theme.

## Marble bathrooms

Many varieties of stone and brick are available and are an interesting addition to the bath because of their various colors and textures. They can be used on the floor or the walls, and in combination with other materials, such as tile or wood. Marble, popular for its beautiful veined appearance and smooth surface, is an expensive material that is often used to convey an aura of wealth and splendor.

Marble, however, is easily stained and rather fragile. Synthetic marble that is practical, easier to install and less expensive is available.

*Photo courtesy of Kohler Co.*

**This tub, encased in marble,** *includes such extras as additional space at one end, which can be used for seating or for conveniently storing accessories. A long marble shelf built flush against the wall also provides room for extra storage.*

**Here the entire bath** has been covered with marble, including the walls, floor and bathing area. Surrounding the room with this one element conveys an image of elegance and richness.

*Seen from the inside* of this luxurious shower, marble walls enclose the stall with smooth stone, while a marble bench allows you to sit while showering. The same colored marble can be seen covering the rest of the bath as well.

**A deep green marble** console sink is set up with bright brass fixtures, adding flair to its already rich surface. This combination fills the room with warmth and grandeur.

**In this room,** two distinct marble patterns complement each other. Dark marble contrasts with a lighter tan stone, providing a fitting background for this room's other distinctive features.

# Ceramic tile

Ceramic tile is the most commonly chosen bathroom material, because it is easy to clean, water-resistant and long lasting. Available in a variety of colors and patterns, ceramic tile offers all sorts of decorating possibilities.

You can combine patterns or use different colors for contrast. Best of all, ceramic is easy to maintain, a plus when it comes to cleaning up.

*This photo and photo on opposite page courtesy of Color Tile, Inc.*

**Simple blue tiles** *are used throughout this room, providing just one pattern and color. This effect is achieved by covering the porcelain tub and vanity with these tiles as well as the ceiling, walls and floor. Along with the appliances, a few well-placed flowers offset the heavy blue, adding diversion with a lighter color and an entirely different texture.*

*Photo courtesy of American Olean Tile Company*

**Tile in one color** *is used on the floor of this room, while another color, in a different style and size, has been placed on the wall. The contrast of both color and pattern adds excitement to the room.*

***Several styles of tile*** *are used in this bath. Large white squares outlined in black cover the floor, while smaller pink tiles trimmed with accent tiles of black and blue are set around the tub. Finally, mosaics made up of all these tiles have been arranged on the wall above, adding a unique visual element.*

***Again we see a variety of tiles*** *in complementary patterns and sizes working together to create an interesting room. Large and small diamonds, black against white, are used with tiny white and black squares, each complementing the other to create a stunning overall effect.*

Photos courtesy of American Olean Tile Company

**An arresting combination of black and gray tiles** *gives this bathing area a pristine atmosphere. Contrast can be provided with accessories; in this case, red and black towels on the wall and a dark green plant set next to the tub.*

**Blue and white tiles** *make up this room, again in various patterns. Here the small blue squares are used exclusively as trim, while diamonds cover the floor and larger squares highlight the expanse of counter space.*

137

# Wood

Wood is a popular choice for bathroom cabinetry but can also be used for appliances, walls, ceilings and floors. It is durable and, if properly treated, stain-resistant; it also adds warmth to a room often outfitted with materials of a colder nature. There are a number of synthetic woods available, including oak, glued planks and butcher block, that are also durable and often just as pleasing to the eye as natural wood.

Photos courtesy of Kraftmaid Cabinetry, Inc.

**In this bath,** oak cabinets in a variety of shapes and sizes are combined with a vanity base in the same pattern. A hardwood floor and wooden siding and trim extend the decor of this warm and friendly room.

**Wooden cabinets** are easy to install and come in a variety of styles. This cabinet features extra shelf space above and below the cupboard itself, providing additional storage.

**This exquisite vanity** is an example of wood used to create an object of great beauty. Delicately carved, the surface is highly polished to emphasize the wood's natural grain. The mirror on the wall above repeats the vanity's pattern and combines with it for a striking and elegant effect.

# Appliances

One easy way to highlight your bathroom is through your choice of appliances and fixtures. Available in a range of styles from classic to modern, these items allow you to fine-tune your bath, complementing your choice of material and color and elaborating on your basic bathroom theme. Highlights include basic appliances, such as the toilet, washbasin and tub, as well as extras like towel racks and soap dishes. Light fixtures are also a great way to add style to your bath.

Highlights other than appliances can be chosen for their flexibility as well as functionality. They are easily changed without much expense, letting you turn a room once meant for a child into one more suitable for a preteen. It doesn't take many of these items to promote style or convey a theme. Notice how various highlights make a statement about each of these rooms.

**Demonstrating old-fashioned appliances** combined with up-to-date style, this tub provides the best of both worlds. Smooth white porcelain rests on a dark oval base, while brass fixtures for both the tub and sink bring the two elements together. Handrails on either end of the tub add function with an extra touch of elegance.

**This delicately curved sink** is lovely enough to become this bathroom's focal point. Taking up little space, it would make a great addition to a smaller bath, providing an example of lots of style in a small package.

**Toilet and matching pedestal sink** are made of textured tile, adding an unusual visual and textural element to this bath.

**The appliances in this room** glow from the light coming in from the windows above the yellow walls. The sink is trimmed with gold, as are the various fixtures on the appliances and the walls, adding to the room's unique coloring.

## Fixtures

Fixtures come in a variety of styles and materials, and cover everything from faucets and door handles to cup holders and light covers. Whether you choose ceramic knobs, sleek chrome faucets or bright brass handrails, these additions give depth to the design of your bath.

***This unique shower enclosure*** *offers aesthetic appeal in a highly technical setting. Shower heads, hand sprays, body sprays and other components allow a variety of showering options, from a fine mist to a soothing massage.*

**Designed along Victorian lines,** this room contains an old-fashioned toilet with a wooden seat and wooden water tank set up high along the wall. A heavy porcelain pedestal sink repeats the design of the porcelain toilet. Brass fixtures are another fine feature in this handsome bath.

**In this room** a wall-mount lavatory and cistern are a unique addition to the bath. They offer an appliance option reminiscent of an earlier and more elegant era.

# Vanities

Vanities come in a variety of shapes, colors and styles and can be used to complement or elaborate upon your bathroom theme. They can be modern, mirrored and freestanding, or Queen Anne style with lots of cabinet space.

Vanities provide the perfect place to take care of your personal needs in peace. Consider introducing one in your bath and making it your own special place to prepare for the upcoming day or unwind before going to bed at night.

**This vanity** is set up with all the items necessary for personal care: a lamp for direct light, an oval mirror hung directly above the sink, natural light from the window, lots of cupboards and drawers beneath and, best of all, plenty of counter space.

**Featuring a comfortable chair** set next to the vanity, this lovely powder room is ready for its occupant to settle in for a quiet hour of grooming. This room has been designed as a special place of retreat, making it perfect to come to at the end of a hectic day.

**Bathrooms with vanities** that connect to the bedroom offer easy access for taking care of personal needs. This vanity provides plenty of counter space, allowing room for spreading out toiletries. Its curves duplicate those of the tub, making it visually consistent with the rest of the room.

# A Portfolio of Bathroom Ideas

# Charming Country-style Bathrooms

What gives a bathroom country style? Is it the clawfoot tub, the antique fixtures, the wooden panelling or the braided rug set in the middle of the floor?

All of these features, as well as many others, can be found in the country bath. These rooms have a rustic edge. They make use of items commonly considered old-fashioned; everything from wicker chairs to tall wooden cabinets once used as wardrobes.

Consider what it is about the following rooms that give them a country feel. You might want to think of ways you can add to this theme, letting your special touch bring to life this favorite decorating scheme.

**This room is truly rugged,** with its chinked log walls and old-fashioned tub. Accessories play an important part in maintaining the theme of this cabin bath: antlers above the sink and fishing tackle next to old work boots set beneath a wooden, straight-backed chair secure the country focus of this room.

**White paneled walls,** an old-fashioned tub, a lovely hardwood cabinet and comfortable chintz chair represent the obvious elements that give this room a country air. Sun pouring in from the window completes the picture in this well-appointed bath.

**Country style** can be evoked with just a few items, like this simple oval mirror in a thin gold frame and the two tiny lamps nestled on either side. Old-fashioned pictures in heavy wooden frames add to the motif.

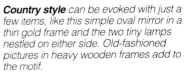

**All the features** you might expect to find in a country bath can be seen in this room: tall wooden cabinets, old-fashioned fixtures above the sink and corresponding accessories, such as small framed pictures grouped together around a simple square mirror. There is even a straight-backed chair tucked under a small wooden vanity.

# Exquisite
# **Romantic**
# Bathrooms

Romantic rooms are places where imagination runs wild and decor leans toward the extraordinary. They make use of extravagant features, often with a sentimental touch. Their colors are usually soft and their edges rounded. Draperies float in the breeze. Romantic rooms can be ornate and richly ornamented or more simply endowed, adorned with a few well-chosen objects.

*This room is a reminder of old-world elegance, with its pillars and statuettes, vines running along the window frame and brightly shining ribbons. A large pedestal sink commands center stage, while an exquisite cut-glass window displaying a simple Grecian figure adds a final fanciful touch.*

**This sink,** *made of vitreous china, is covered with whimsical rabbits in cobalt blue. Accents such as the various jars, dishes and ceramic tiles repeat the design, adding to the lightness of this one small section of the room.*

**This bathroom corner** *features a classical pedestal sink. Heavy draperies tied back with tasseled cord, an intricately crafted mirror and a myriad of ornate accessories work together to suggest extravagance, a common romantic characteristic.*

Photo courtesy of American Olean Tile Company

157

**Dainty curves** *and fluted edges turn this pedestal sink into a work of art. A simple pattern, delicately applied, runs along its edges, adding to its lightness and fragile grace.*

**Peonies and ivy** *cover the inside of this basin, running along ceramic tiles on the wall and repeated on the fixtures. The sink is set inside a curved wooden vanity of deep mahogany, while an ornate Oriental carpet, glimpsed beneath, completes the romantic effect.*

**Pretty pinks** *suffuse this room with warmth and delicate color. Original features include a large, curved iron plant holder and matching settee. Sunlight shines in on a comfortable window seat. Notice the towels tucked into open cupboards set directly into the wall, a creative use of space as well as an interesting decorative feature.*

# Lovely
# **Garden-style**
## Bathrooms

Garden-style bathrooms use natural elements for their theme. Whether cut flowers are set around in vases or climbing vines decorate the appliances, the garden bath has a fresh flavor, reminding us of colorful meadows and newly mown fields.

These bathrooms use natural furnishings, dried flower arrangements, and flowered wallpaper as well as lots of plants in hanging baskets or large pots set on the floor. They are rooms that liven the senses, filling you with a feeling of the outdoors. This theme will always be a bathroom favorite.

*Fish swim* on a sea-green wall above the tub in this garden bath, while a tall, green plant hovers over them, looking like seaweed, and sunlight streams in through the window. Even the wrought-iron chair looks as if it were made from twigs and branches.

***Tiny pink and blue flowers*** *decorate the appliances in this bath, matching a real basket of flowers set to one side. The delicacy of the flowered appliances, combined with bright light from the window, resembles a well-trimmed English garden full of forget-me-nots.*

**Lush green plants** *surround this tub. The base of the tub and the pedestal sink are trimmed with flowers, as if they are sitting in the middle of a garden.*

**This room is filled with flowers,** both natural and painted. A decorative flower design covers the appliances and ceramic tiles, while on the wall above the sink, a mirror reflects the scene. Finally, vases of fresh flowers are set on shelves above the sink and toilet, surrounding the room with freshness.

Photo courtesy of Kohler Co.

**Here a sink and matching accessories,** brightly painted with red and yellow tulips, suggest a garden in spring. They are a lighthearted addition to any bath.

**One wicker chair** and a simple round log, set against the wall to serve as a table, are elements that give this bath a carefree, natural touch. A tall green plant next to the tub and a flowered picture on the wall add to the outdoor flavor of this room.

# Fabulous CONTEMPORARY Bathrooms

The contemporary bath contains up-to-date features in a modern setting. Following current trends, this type of bath is often technologically advanced, filled with state-of-the-art appliances and fashionable highlights. Design is often angular, or along more straightforward lines.

The beauty of this type of bath lies in its simplicity; however, this does not mean it lacks allure. The following rooms are filled with features that enhance their simpler styles.

***This modern bath*** *makes use of appliances built along simple lines that are geometrically shaped. The room is large, containing both a toilet and bidet, a tub and a separate shower stall. In the middle of the room stands the lavatory, complete with a huge mirror and lots of shelf and counter space. Various types of lighting are used, from "fluorescent" bulbs by the mirror to incandescent fixtures above the tub, while from above, a large, square skylight spreads light and shadow across the walls and floor, creating patterns that repeat the room's simple lines.*

Photo courtesy of Kohler Co.

**Tiled steps lead up to a large,** angular tub, this room's main feature. Placed under a glass block wall, the tub is filled with unobstructed sunlight. This window eliminates the need for draperies or other window coverings. A comfortable striped couch occupies one wall of the room, while accents such as candles, a decorative plate and an abstract painting are also used. Notice the angular mirror above the sink, also a contemporary feature.

**This room makes use of rounded edges** and gentle curves, an earlier style that has again become popular. The shell-shaped light fixture above the counter is especially interesting. An arched window set above the tub and across from the vanity is reflected in the mirror's glass.

**Textured pearl gray walls** and bright white appliances are the arresting features in this modern room. The canopy beneath the sink serves as decorative cover for the plumbing.

**The details in this room are elaborate.** *The sink is lined with gold, and gold hardware is used throughout the room. Notice the geometric design at the base of the bidet. Even the legs of the lavatory are distinctively shaped, with intricate knobs capping them off at the top.*

**Light from the window** bounces off this modest washbasin and is reflected back onto the tiny tiles on the wall. The design of the sink is uncomplicated, in keeping with contemporary styles, which prize the plain and unadorned.

Photos courtesy of Kohler Co.

# Distinctive
## Bathrooms

Bathrooms that are distinctive include elements that go beyond what is usually expected in the bath. They are unique, perhaps because their purpose is unusual or because they are filled with extraordinary items.

These kinds of baths lift us beyond our expectations to delightful, even exhilarating heights. They stretch the imagination, making us think of exciting possibilities we might not otherwise have considered. Set your imagination free as you explore the unusual elements of these remarkable rooms.

## Family

Bathrooms that are used by an entire family, no matter how many people this includes, should be designed to meet a variety of needs. Consider the following if you are designing this type of bath: Is there enough room? Is it easy to care for, and does it provide privacy? Can it accommodate both genders? Will children be using it? What about company?

The family bath, although needing to be efficient, does not have to be limited by this need. Have fun when designing this type of room. Be creative, considering the personalities of those who will be using it. Ask for their ideas. The family bath will see lots of action; make it friendly as well as practical.

Photos courtesy of National Kitchen & Bath Association; project designed by Shelley Patterson, L. Jones

**Suited to meet the needs of both sexes,** this room provides plenty of space without a loss of privacy. The tub is hidden behind a curved wall of glass block, while linen is stored in a separate section that doubles as a dressing area. There is even enough room for the morning cup of coffee!

Photos on this page courtesy of Grohe America

**Two sinks,** two mirrors, a toilet, a bidet and the traditional enclosed tub-and-shower combination make this bright blue bathroom a family favorite. Completely tiled and easy to clean, it sets the standard for any family bath.

**Featuring bright colors and bold patterns,** this child's bathroom has been built with appliances that are low to the ground and easy to reach. The shower, set up with a detachable nozzle, makes washing up painless and quick.

**Sporting two sinks,** lots of cupboards, shelves and drawers, a large tub and, most important of all, plenty of floor space, this bathroom is perfect for a family of any size. An added plus is the unlimited availability of light; fixtures have been placed in such a way that light can be shed on all the main areas of activity.

# Distinctive Bathrooms
## Workout

Many people have added exercise to their daily routine and are faced with the problem of storing equipment that is utilized every day, but only for limited periods of time. One solution is letting the bathroom double as a private workout facility.

Adding exercise equipment to the bath is an easy way to include this important activity to your routine and offers the added convenience of a ready shower when the workout is through. It also lets you store your workout equipment in a room where it will be out of the way when not in use.

**Both a rowing machine and an exercise bike** fit into this large bathroom area. One of them was placed in the hall outside the main room to save on space, a unique storage idea.

**This bath contains** enough room for stretching out before starting the workout. The exercise bike has been set in a corner, where it occupies little room and does not detract from the main bathing area.

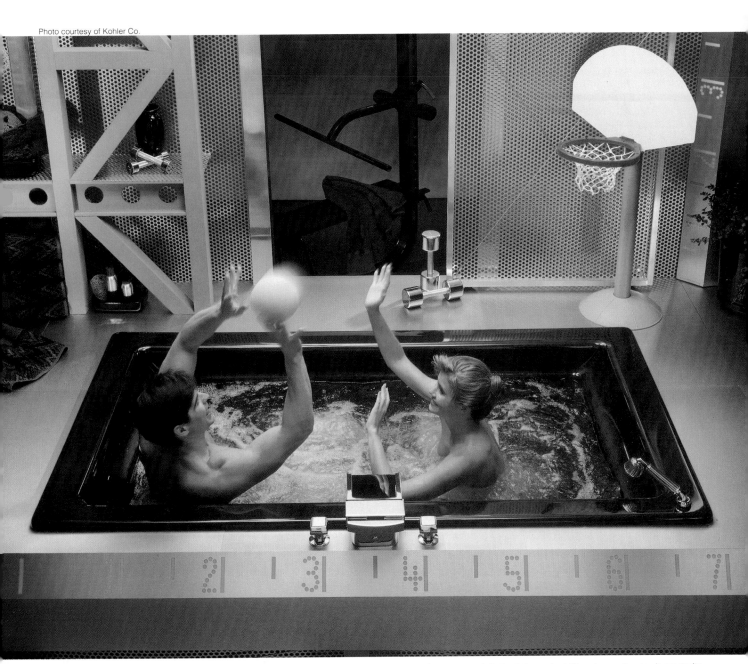

**In this creative bath,** the whirlpool doubles as a basketball court. There is room enough for two people in the tub, and additional exercise equipment sits outside the bathing area, which has been designed to look like a playing field.

# Distinctive Bathrooms
## Deluxe

Rich in style and comfort, the following rooms contain everything from fireplaces and overstuffed armchairs to television sets. Deluxe bathrooms have lavish features that make them luxurious. Filled with an abundance suggestive of great wealth, some contain duplicate matching appliances, while others provide intricate decorations or a variety of comfortable amenities.

Deluxe baths contain original designs in elaborate settings. Enjoy the following rooms; even if you do not aspire to this type of setting for your own bath, you can still take pleasure in their splendor and find inspiration in their elaborate decor.

*Rich in style and comfort,* this room contains everything from a fireplace, comfortable chairs and softly lit lamps to a recessed bathing area with a shower stall on one side and a separate room for the toilet on the other. These are set off from the main room by curtained panels in a delicate floral print while the vanity resides in the middle of the room. A sink sits on one side, counter space is available on the other and a mirror has been hung in the middle. This is truly a magnificent room.

Photo courtesy of Armstrong World Industries, Inc.

**The pleasures of television** have been added to this bath with not one, but two, T.V.'s set in the wall above a built-in shelf, a convenient way to catch up on the morning news on different channels! Again we see rolled towels set into an open cupboard area. A long shelf has been built next to the sink, where several odds and ends are conveniently stored.

**Here a triangular shower stall,** *occupying one corner of the bath, takes up little room but is a perfect place for two to shower in comfort. This roomy stall is designed with two shower heads and two sets of faucets, ending the debate over how hot or cold the shower should be.*

**Perfect for the powder room,** this Queen Anne style double-basin vanity is designed for convenience as well as beauty. Built of hardwood with a china basin, polished brass faucets and lots of storage space, it is set off with the addition of matching framed mirrors and twin wall-mounted lamps.

**A washbasin** lined with strips of gold brightens this sink area, while matching fixtures add an extra burst of luxury.

**Spaciousness dominates this room,** *allowing the functional features to blend into the background. The room includes a black tub and black double washbasins, an arched window set high above the sink with matching arched beams in the middle of the room, padded seats, lots of cupboards and plenty of windows covered with vertical blinds. Small, square rust-colored tiles cover the floor and lead up to the tub, filling the room with their warm, polished glow.*

# Distinctive Bathrooms
## Exotic

Exotic bathrooms are filled with sensational and elaborate props. They invite us to indulge in a world of make-believe where we can inhabit our dreams, even if only for a time.

Making use of unusual appliances, original combinations and novel structures, they suggest a place where fantasy becomes reality and where the unexpected is customary.

As with the deluxe bathroom, while you might never create a bath as elaborate as these, you can still appreciate their originality and perhaps be inspired to include an exotic element in your own bath.

*First to grab the eye* in this unique bath is a thin, freestanding black wall set in the middle of the room, serving as both a room divider and a background for the sink and mirror. Behind it sit the toilet and bidet; in front are an overstuffed armchair and footstool. Steps lead up to the ceramic tub, while the impression of an old-world garden is evoked by stone planters filled with climbing vines.

***Serene blue and simple white*** on the walls and floor are a fitting background to this bath, with its carved pillars and dazzling white lavatory molded from a single ceramic piece. Tall palms wave in the background behind the curved tub, while natural light is diffused throughout the room.

**An Oriental pattern** in sculpted green waves drapes across this china basin, while black and gold accents add extra elegance.

**This exotic wooden vanity,** reminiscent of Far Eastern furnishings, adds an unusual touch to this bath. Its features include a black octagonal basin and plenty of drawer and counter space. A zebra skin, serving as a rug, adds additional foreign flair to the room.

*In an unusual turn of events,* two wrought-iron chairs, a settee with golden tassels and a gilt-framed mirror set the tone for this oval room, while the large pedestal sink and claw-foot tub in the background serve as accompaniments. Blue pin-striped wallpaper and a powder blue curtain knotted and draped across the room add flair and individuality.

Photos on this page courtesy of Kohler Co.

**Flowers fill this sink,** merging together at the bottom as if from a single plant. The basin is set in a green marble console, while the handles are trimmed with the same flower design and set on either side of an antique polished-brass faucet.

Photo courtesy of Armstrong World Industries, Inc.

**Console tables** provide counter space without taking up room. This elaborate design, set directly into the wall, is made of marble with antique faucets of polished brass and elaborately carved wrought-iron legs.

# Distinctive Bathrooms
## Special needs

**The tub in this room** allows easy access with its hinged door and built-in handrail. The door to the tub seals tight inside, preventing the possibility of leakage. Just walk in, close the door and turn on the water! The toilet is wheelchair-accessible, and the wide sink, jutting out past the counter's edge, is within easy reach from a sitting position.

Recently bathrooms designed with appliances and fixtures that meet the needs of those who are physically challenged have become widely available. Not simply utilitarian, these rooms are attractive and inviting places featuring customized appliances that are pleasant to look at while providing independence for those with special needs.

**Providing such features** as an adjustable sink able to accommodate a wheelchair and a comfortable folding seat in the shower area, this room has handrails placed next to the toilet for added support and easy-to-use faucets and fixtures. Wood panelling and a wood-framed mirror add a rustic element to this pleasant, yet functional, room.

# LIST OF CONTRIBUTORS

We'd like to thank the following companies for providing the photographs used in this book:

**American Olean Tile Company**
1000 Cannon Avenue
Dept. BD
Lansdale, PA 19446-0271
215-393-2237

**American Standard**
1 Centennial Plaza
Piscataway, NJ 08855
For the free guide book, We Want
You to Love Your Bathroom, call
1-800-524-9797

**Andersen Windows, Inc.**
P.O. Box 3900
Peoria, IL 61614
1-800-426-4261

**Armstrong World Industries, Inc.**
P.O. Box 3001
Lancaster, PA 17604
1-800-233-3823

**Bates & Bates**
3699 Industry Ave.
Lakewood, CA 90712
1-800-726-7680

**Color Tile, Inc.**
515 Houston St.
Fort Worth, TX 76102
1-800-688-8063
Over 800 Color Tile and Carpet
locations coast to coast. Check
the white pages of your telephone
directory for the one nearest you.

**Congoleum Corporation**
3705 Quakerbridge Rd.
Mercerville, NJ 08619
1-800-934-3567

**Crystal Cabinet Works, Inc.**
1100 Crystal Drive
Princeton, MN 55371
612-389-4187

**Dura Supreme**
300 Dura Drive
Howard Lake, MN 55349
612-543-3872

**Gallop Studios**
Suite 103
2500 Broadway St. N.E.
Minneapolis, MN 55343
612-379-8040

**Grohe America**
241 Covington Drive
Bloomingdale, IL 60108
708-582-7711

**KitchenAid Inc.**
Whirlpool Corporation
Consumer Services
2303 Pipestone Road
Benton Harbor, MI 49022-2400
1-800-422-1230

**Kitchens & Baths by Lynn**
Lynn Wallace, CKD
44489 Town Center Way,
Ste. D254
Palm Desert, CA 92260
1-800-556-LYNN

**Kitchens & Baths by Design**
David Skomsvold, designer
5276A Scotts Valley Drive
Scotts Valley, CA 95066
408-438-1843

**Kohler Co.**
Kohler, WI 53044
1-800-4-KOHLER

**KraftMaid Cabinetry, Inc.**
16052 Industrial Parkway
Middlefield, OH 44062
1-800-654-3008

**Lehmann & Jones Kitchen Studio**
Karen Lehmann, ASID, CKD
612-927-4444

**Merillat Industries, Inc.**
P.O. Box 1946
Adrian, MI 49221
517-263-0771

**National Kitchen & Bath Association**
687 Willow Grove Street
Hackettstown, NJ 07840
1-800-THE-NKBA

**Porcher Ltd.**
3618 E. LaSalle St.
Phoenix, AZ 85040
1-800-338-1756

**Quaker Maid, div. WCI, Inc.**
Rte. 61
Leesport, PA 19533
215-926-3011

**Stained Glass Overlay of St. Paul/Minneapolis**
Suite 9
2660 Cleveland Ave. N.
Roseville, MN 55113
612-628-0308

**Triangle Pacific Corp.**
16803 Dallas Parkway
Dallas, TX 75248
214-931-3000

**WILSONART/Ralph Wilson Plastics Company**
600 South General Bruce Drive
Temple, TX 76504
817-778-2711

**Wood-Mode Cabinetry, Inc.**
No. 1, 2nd Street
Kreamer, PA 17833
717-374-2711